Kama Sutra

DOT-TO-DOT

◨ SQUARE PEG

Kama is love, pleasure and sensual gratification ... the Sutra, is a rule or aphorism in Sanskrit literature. The Kama Sutra, therefore, means The Rules of Love, Pleasure and Sensual Gratification

bird position

Lotus position

Leaning back
or reclining, the
woman crosses
her legs in the
lotus position and
lifts her thighs to
meet her breasts.
And then, in a
kneeling or lying
position, thus
the man enters her.

the splitting of a bamboo

'When the woman places one of
her legs on her lover's shoulder, and
stretches the other out, and then
places the latter on his shoulder, and
stretches out the other, and continues
to do so alternately, it is called the
"splitting of a bamboo".'
Kama Sutra

exchanging energy position

'The inner heart spreads
out in a self-kindled glow.
Externally this manifests
in a vermilion-like light
that surrounds the body;
internally it is a five-coloured
radiant energy that is
emitted and spread out in
lines, like the tense string
of a bow, vibrating silently.'
Six Yogas of Naropa

38

37 •

36 •

35 •

kneeling position

the cow

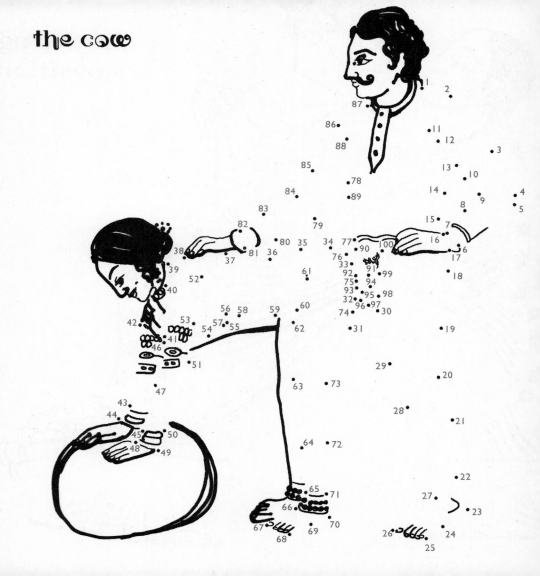

'When a woman stands on her
hands and feet like a quadruped,
and her lover mounts her like a bull,
it is called the "congress of a cow".
At this time everything that is
ordinarily done on the bosom
should be done on the back.'
Kama Sutra

standing position

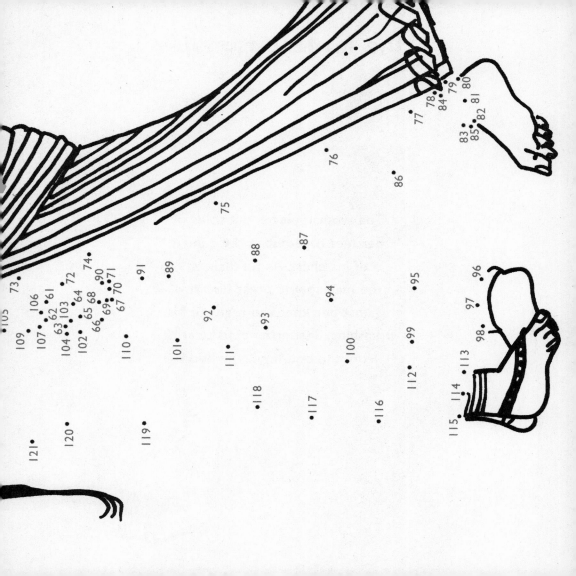

the tantric tortoise

The woman places the soles of
her feet together in the centre
of his chest. As he thrusts,
the man should press his arms
against her knees to regulate his
breathing. Best attempted starting
from the one-leg-up position.

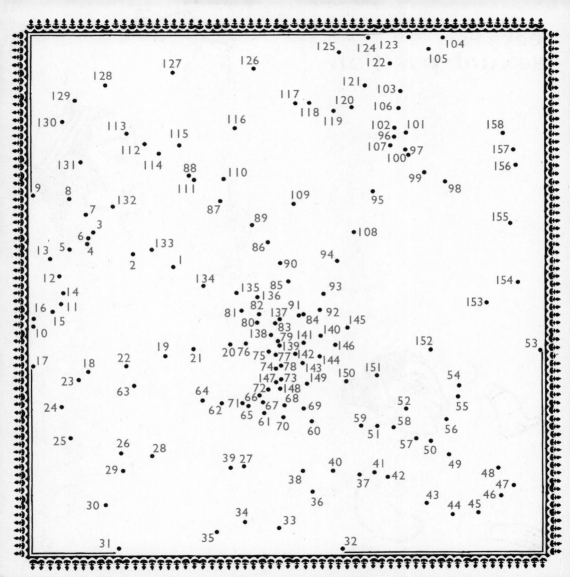

reverse
sexual position

solar lunar breathing position

'The union of man and woman is like
the mating of Heaven and Earth.
It is because of their correct mating
that Heaven and Earth last forever.
Humans have lost this secret and have
therefore become mortal. By knowing
it the Path to Immortality is opened.'
Shang-ku-San-Tai

the Lock

'Females, from their consciousness
of desire, feel a certain kind of
pleasure, which gives them satisfaction,
but it is impossible for them to tell
you what kind of pleasure they feel.
The fact from which this becomes
evident is, that males, when engaged
in coition, cease of themselves after
emission, and are satisfied, but it
is not so with females.'
Kama Sutra

prolonging ecstasy position

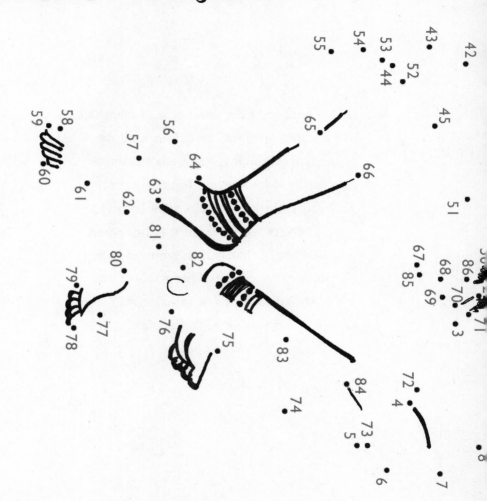

glorious position

'When a woman sees that her lover
is fatigued by constant congress,
without having his desire satisfied,
she should, with his permission,
lay him down upon his back, and give
him assistance by acting his part.
She may also do this to satisfy the
curiosity of her lover, or her own
desire of novelty.'
Kama Sutra

fixing a nail

balance position

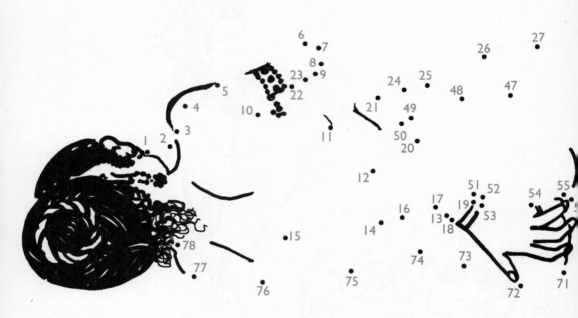

The couple lie facing each other,
straight and on their sides and keep their limbs still.

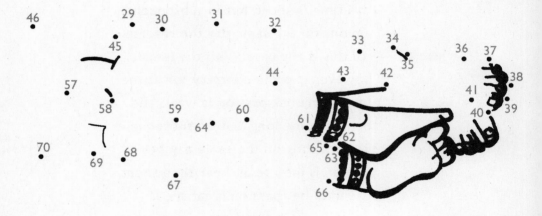

This position, also referred to as double hemisphere,
allows for gentle, rhythmic love making.

tantric love posture

'At the first time of sexual union the
passion of the male is intense, and
his time is short, but in subsequent
unions on the same day the reverse
of this is the case. With the female,
however, it is the contrary, for at the
first time her passion is weak, and
then her time long, but on subsequent
occasions on the same day, her
passion is intense and her time short,
until her passion is satisfied.'

Kama Sutra

the conjunction between sun and moon

The man, seated in the lotus position, takes the woman in his lap so they are closely as one. As they embrace each other's necks, their arms direct the rhythm of their lovemaking.

tantric union

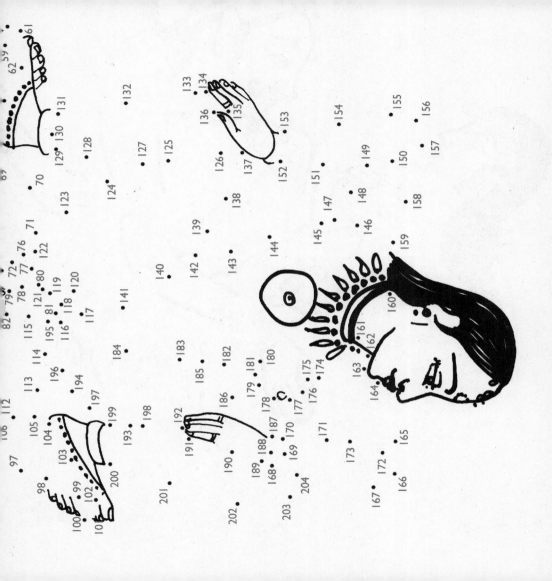

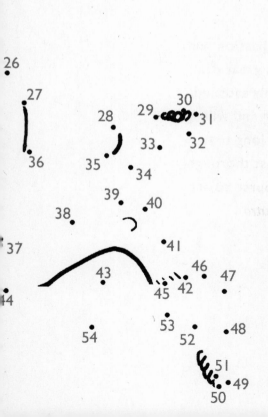

The woman raises
her right leg to rest
on his left shoulder,
and her left leg to his
upper thigh, pressing
tightly against him and
rocking rhythmically.
This position gives rise
to greatly heightened
erotic pleasure for
the couple.

'The strength of passion with
women varies a great deal,
some being easily satisfied,
and others eager and willing
to go on for a long time.
To satisfy these last thoroughly
a man must recourse to art.'
Kama Sutra

the crow

the crab

'When both the legs of the woman are contracted, and placed on her stomach, it is called the "crab's position".'
Kama Sutra

spontaneous and joyous ecstasy position

'As dough is prepared for baking, so must a woman be prepared for sexual intercourse, if she is to derive satisfaction from it.'
Kama Sutra

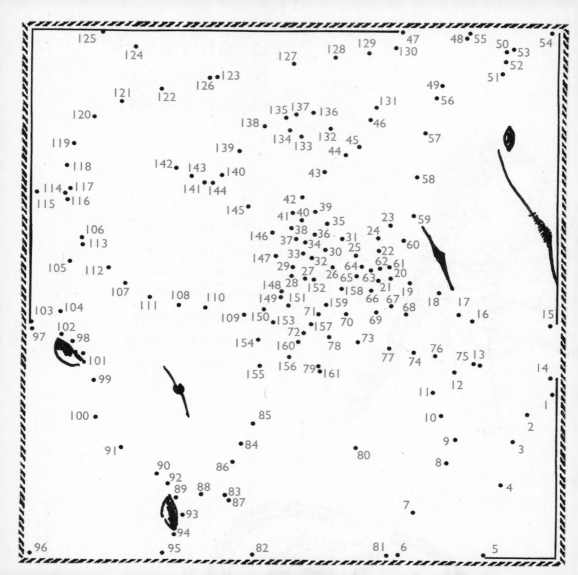

the tortoise

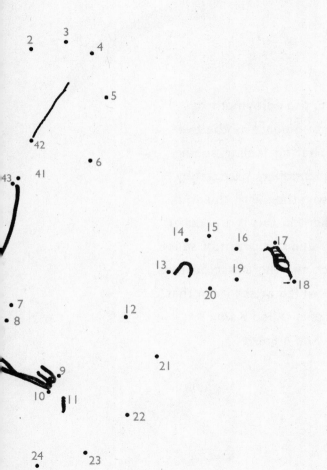

'Eat my essence!
Drink the waters of release!'
Chandamaharosana Tantra

all around position

'Kama is the enjoyment of
appropriate objects by the five
senses of hearing, feeling, seeing,
tasting and smelling, assisted by
the mind together with the soul.
The ingredient in this is a peculiar
contact between the organ of sense
and its object, and the consciousness
of pleasure which arises from that
contact is called Kama.'
Kama Sutra

inverted position

'Though a woman is reserved, and keeps her feelings concealed;
yet when she gets on the top of a man, she then shows all her love
and desire. A man should gather from the actions of the woman of
what disposition she is, and in what way she likes to be enjoyed.'

Kama Sutra

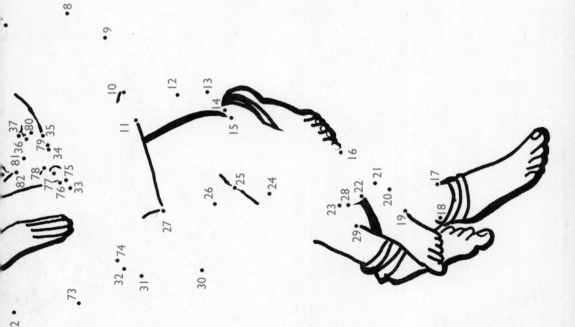

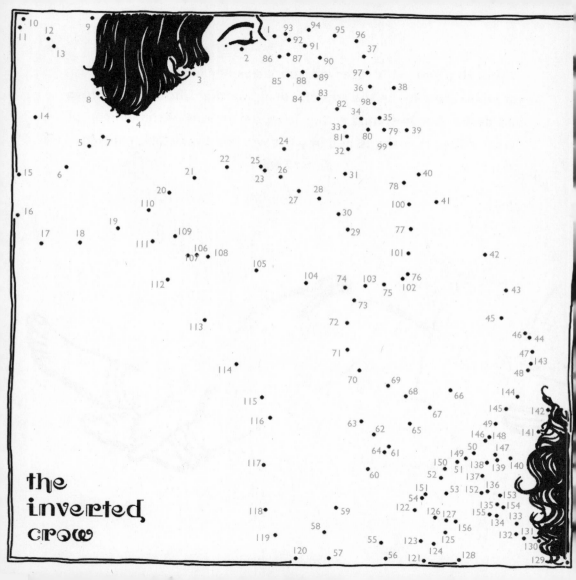

the
inverted
crow

Lotus position

knee and elbow position

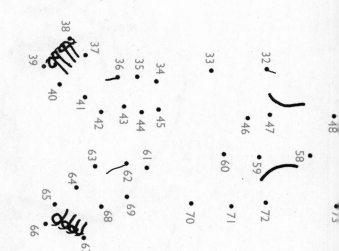

Published by Square Peg 2013

10 9

First published in Great Britain in 2013 by Square Peg
Random House, 20 Vauxhall Bridge Road, London SW1V 2SA

www.vintage-books.co.uk

Addresses for companies within The Random House Group Limited can be found at: www.randomhouse.co.uk/offices.htm

The Random House Group Limited Reg. No. 954009

A CIP catalogue record for this book is available from the British Library

ISBN 978 0 22 409857 1

Printed and bound in India by Thomson Press India Ltd.

Penguin Random House is committed to a sustainable future for
our business, our readers and our planet. This book is made from
Forest Stewardship Council® certified paper.

MIX
Paper from
responsible sources
FSC
www.fsc.org
FSC® C018179